Connect the Dots Activity Book
The Places We'll Go

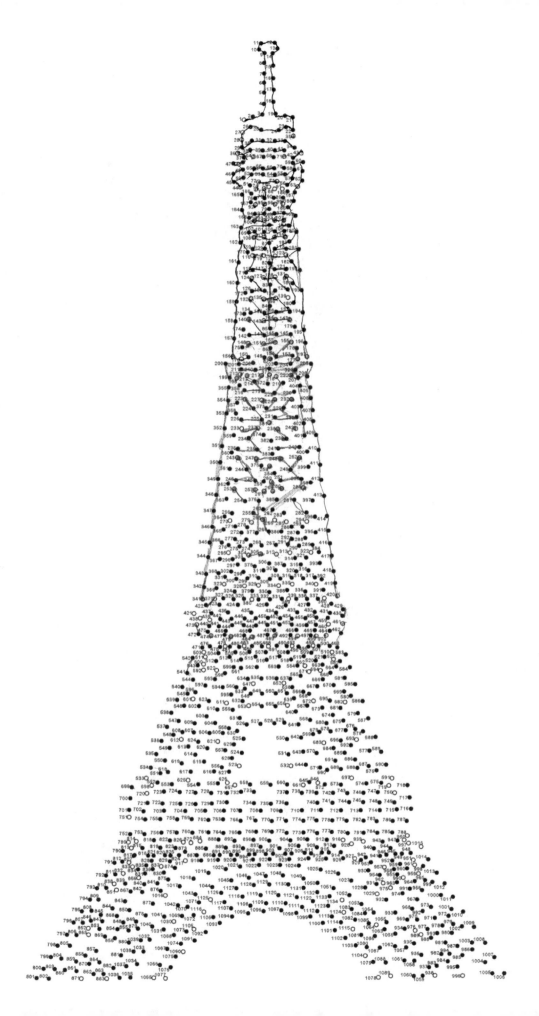

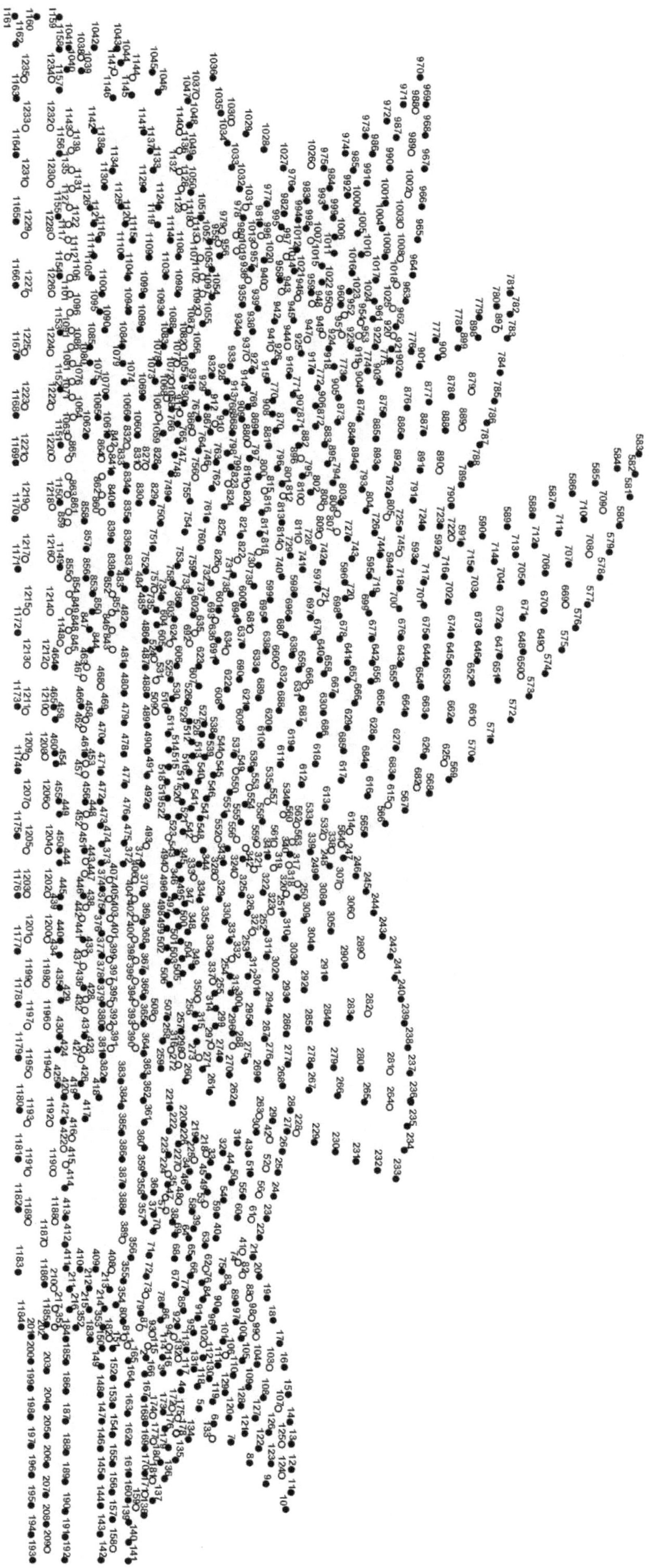

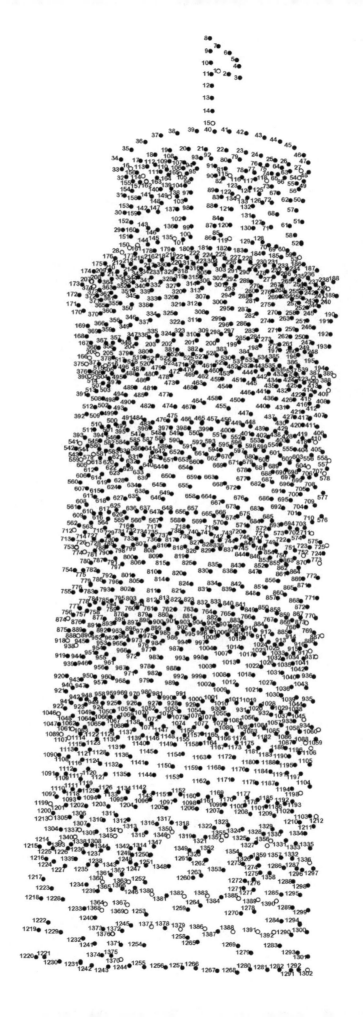

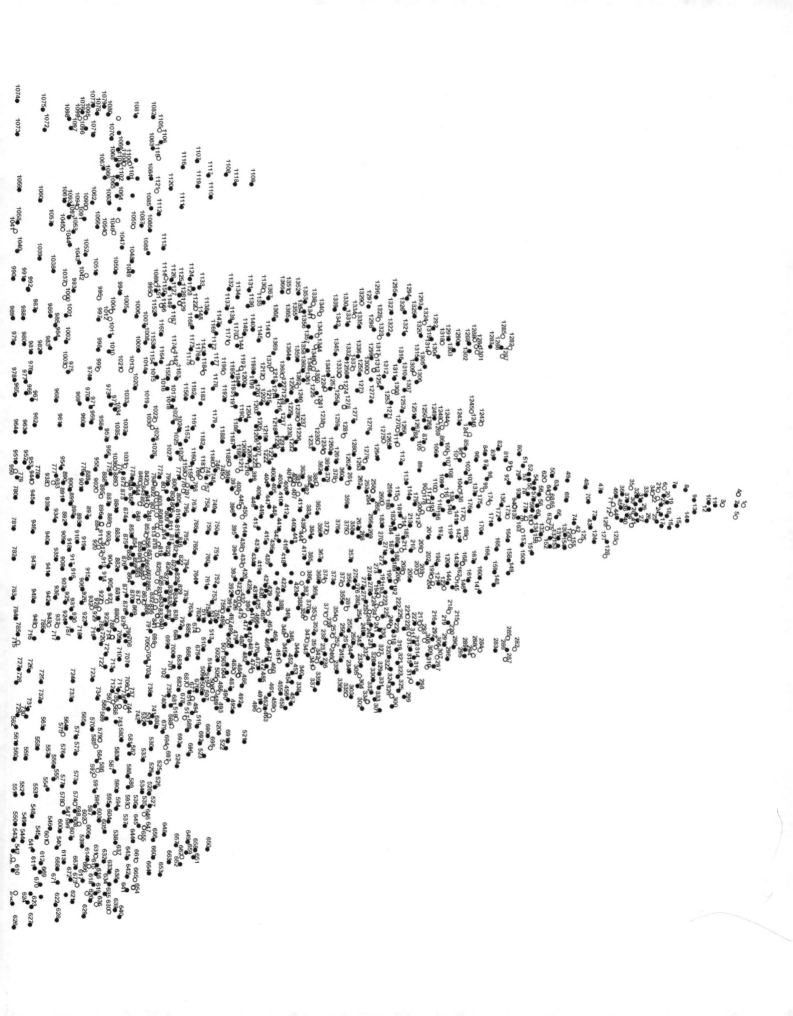

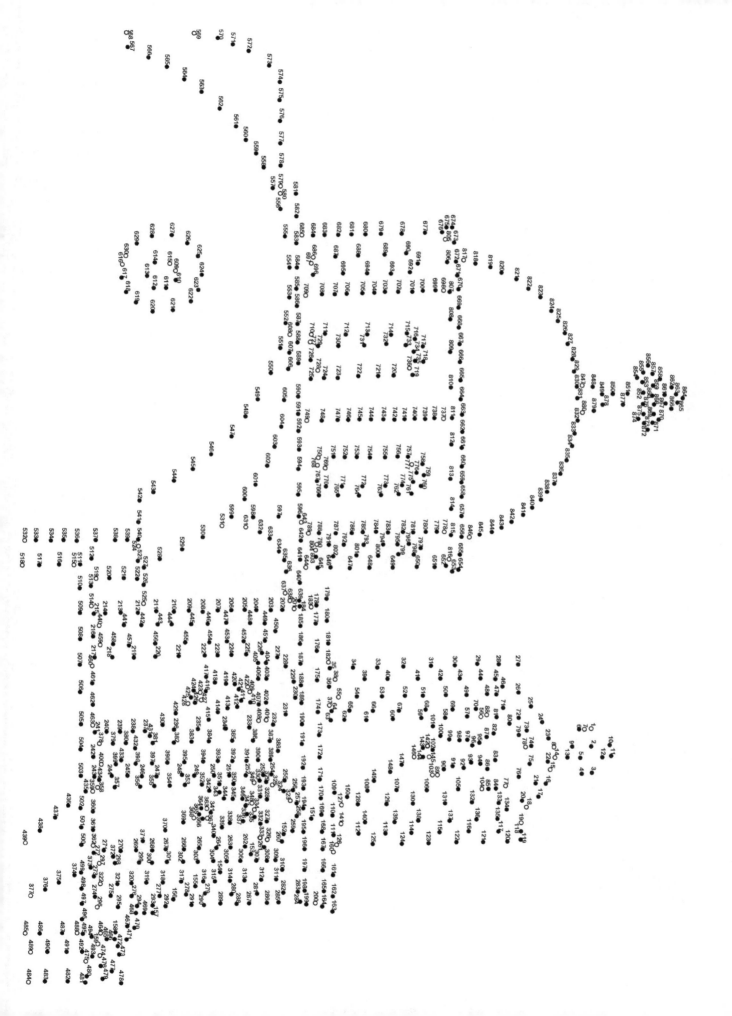

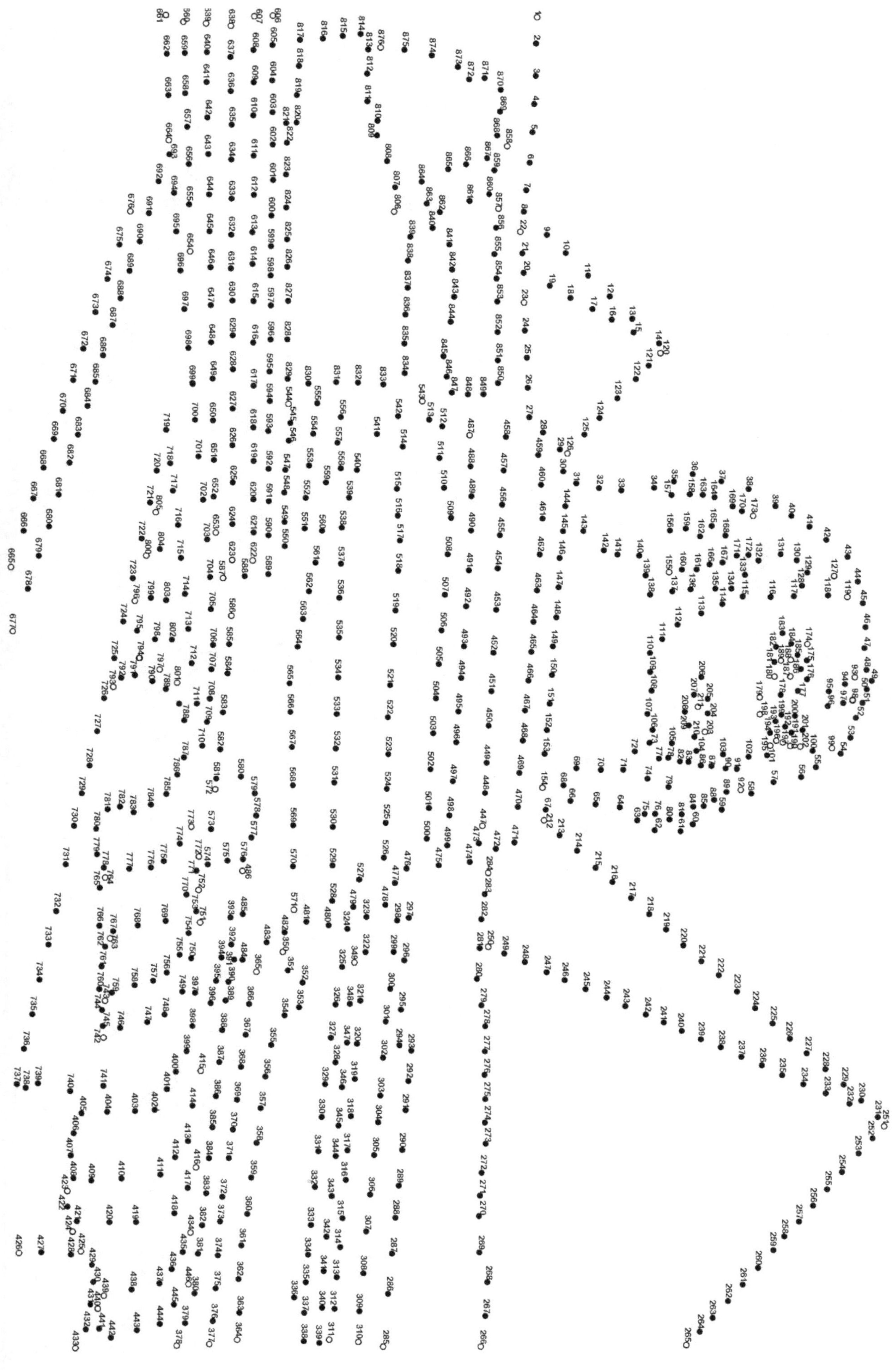

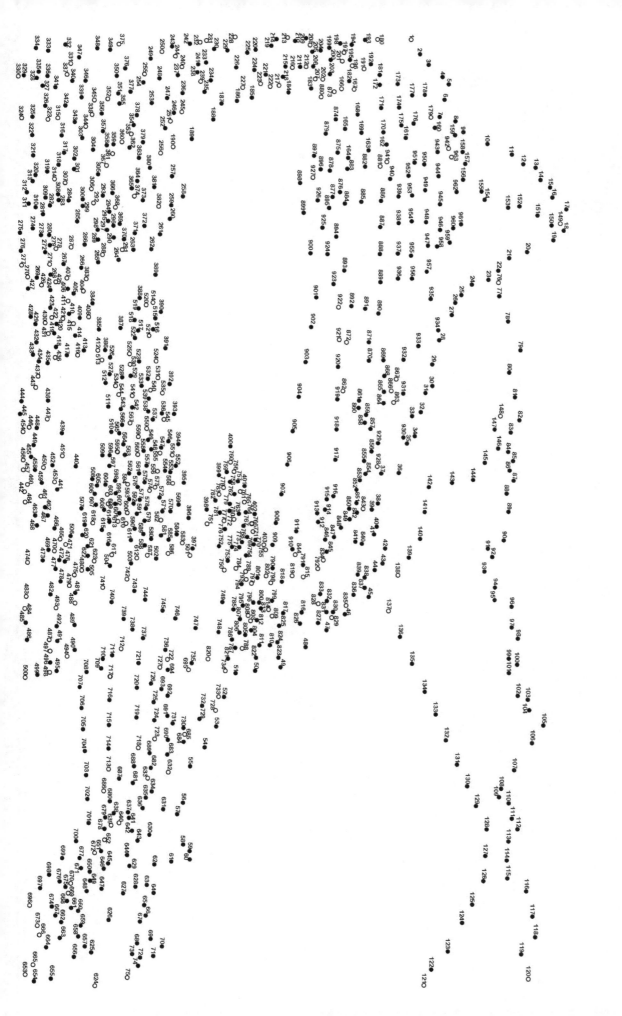

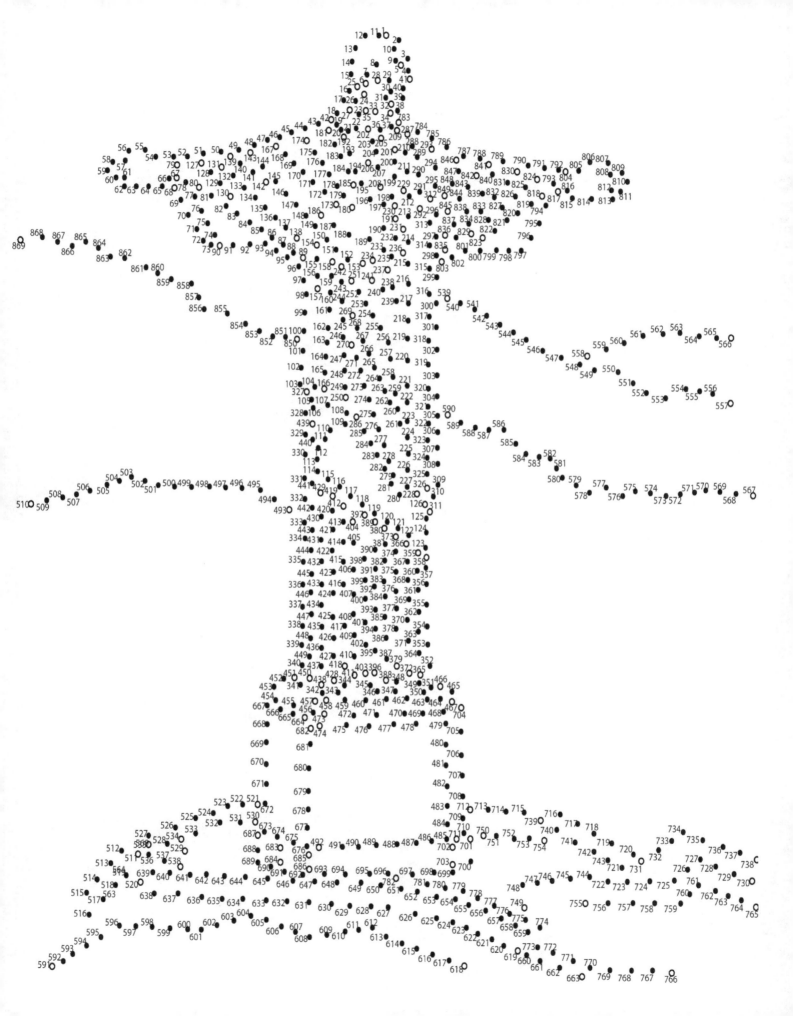

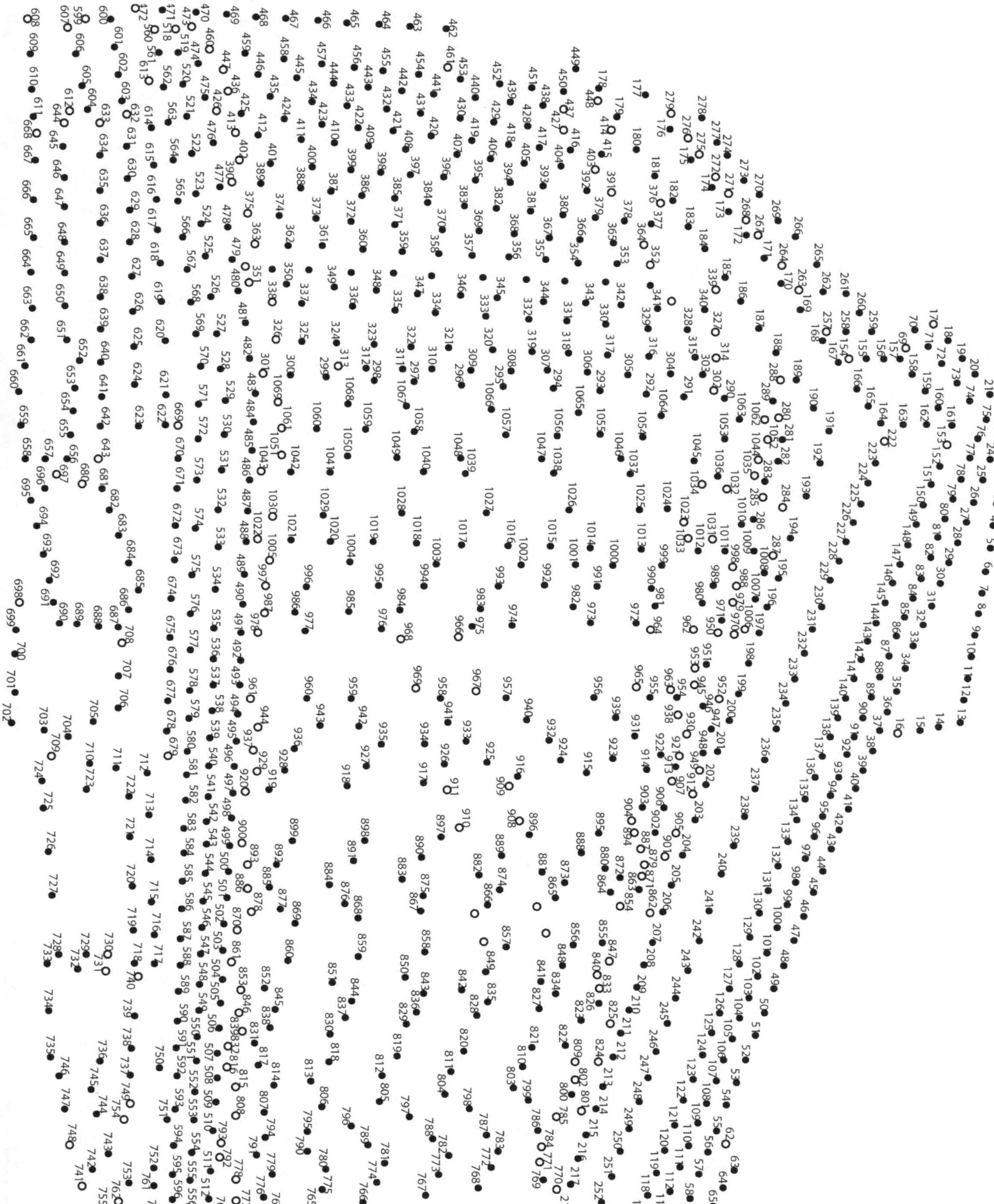

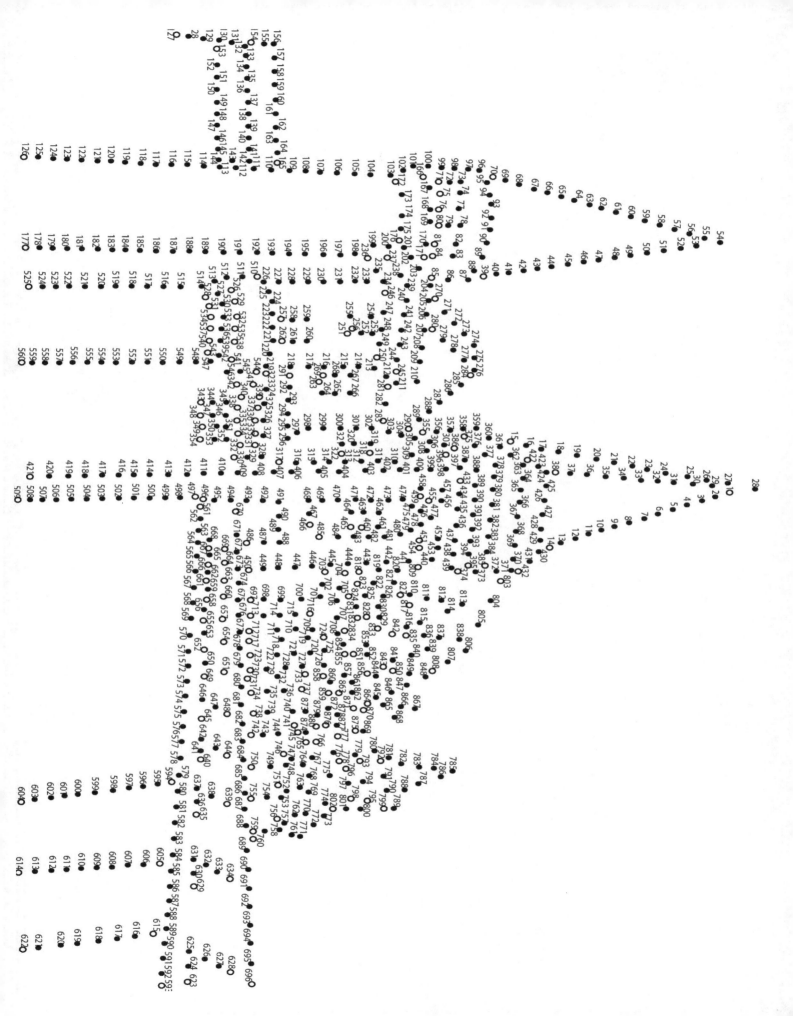

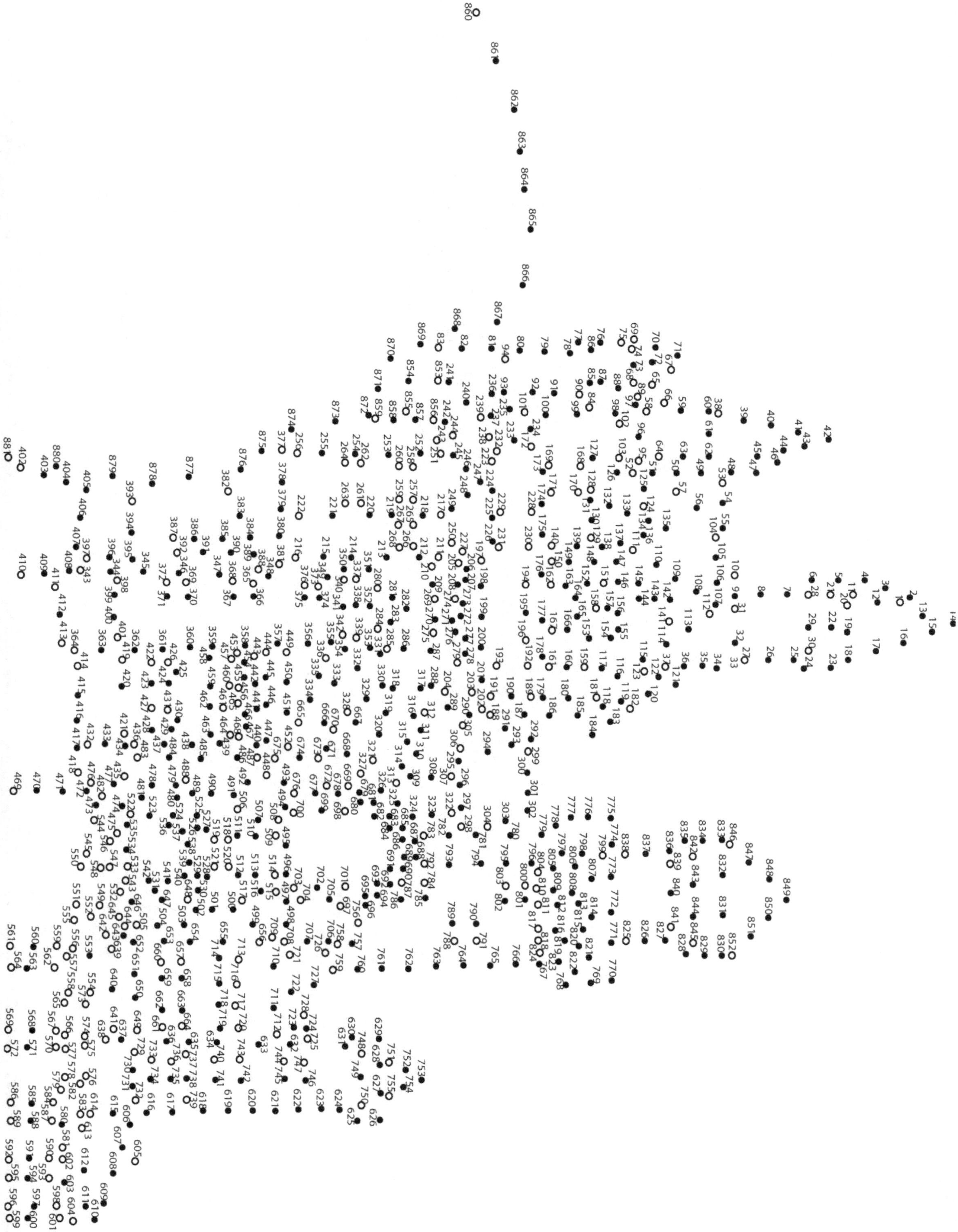

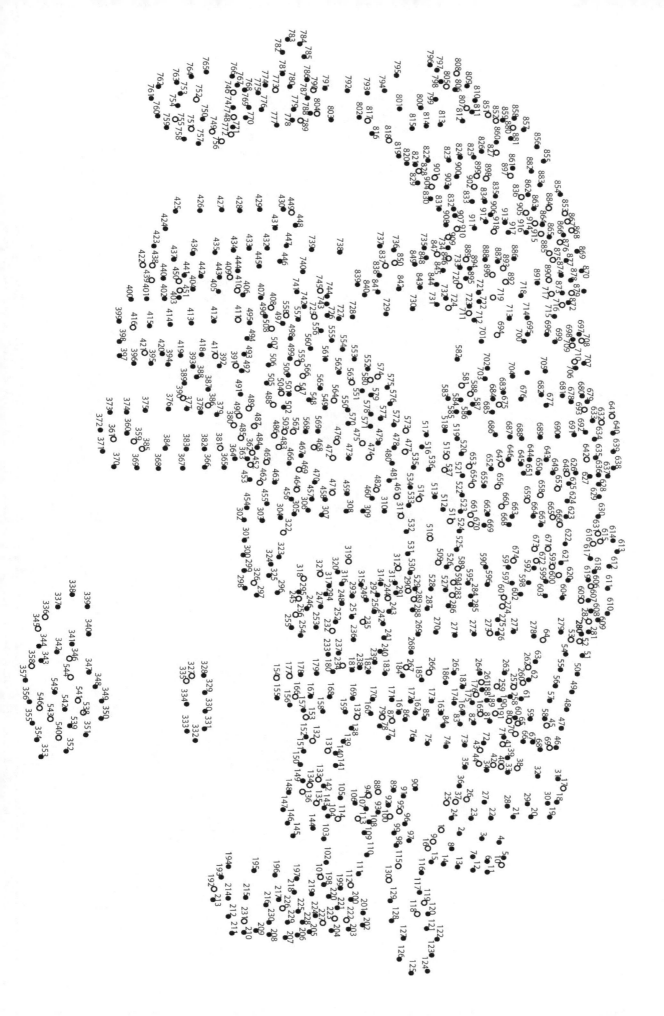

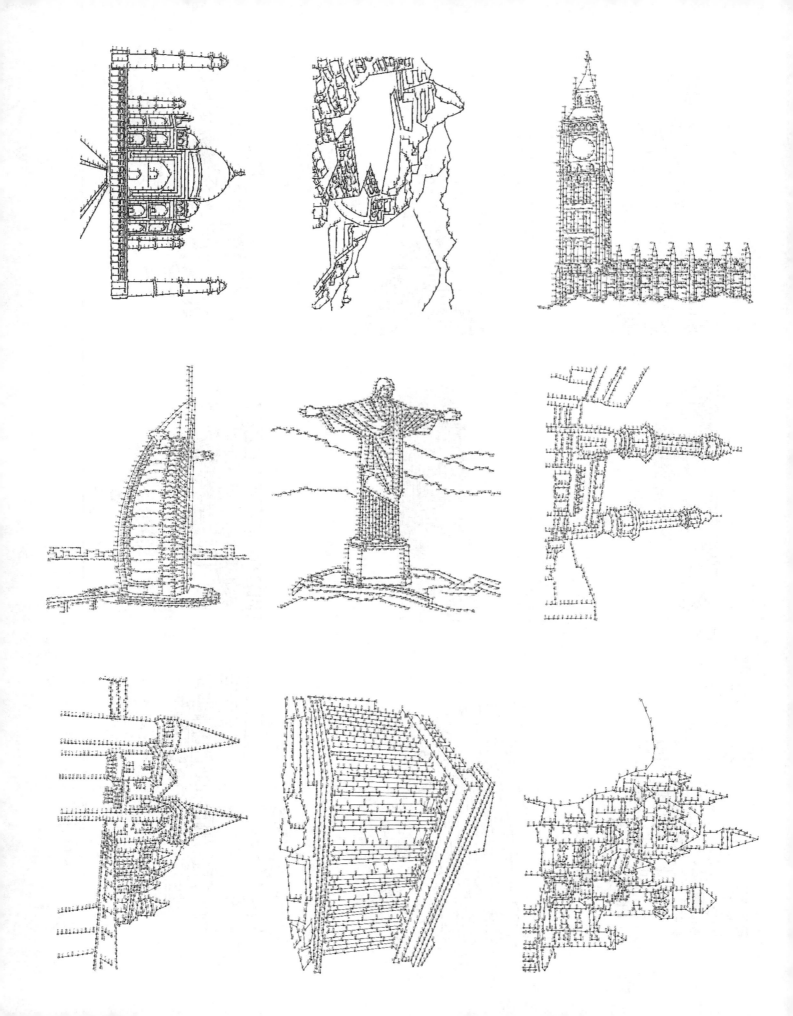

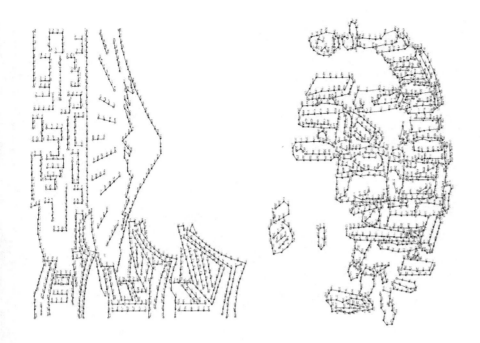

BONUS!

Thank you for purchasing this book, as a bonus, enjoy these mandala dot to dot challenges!

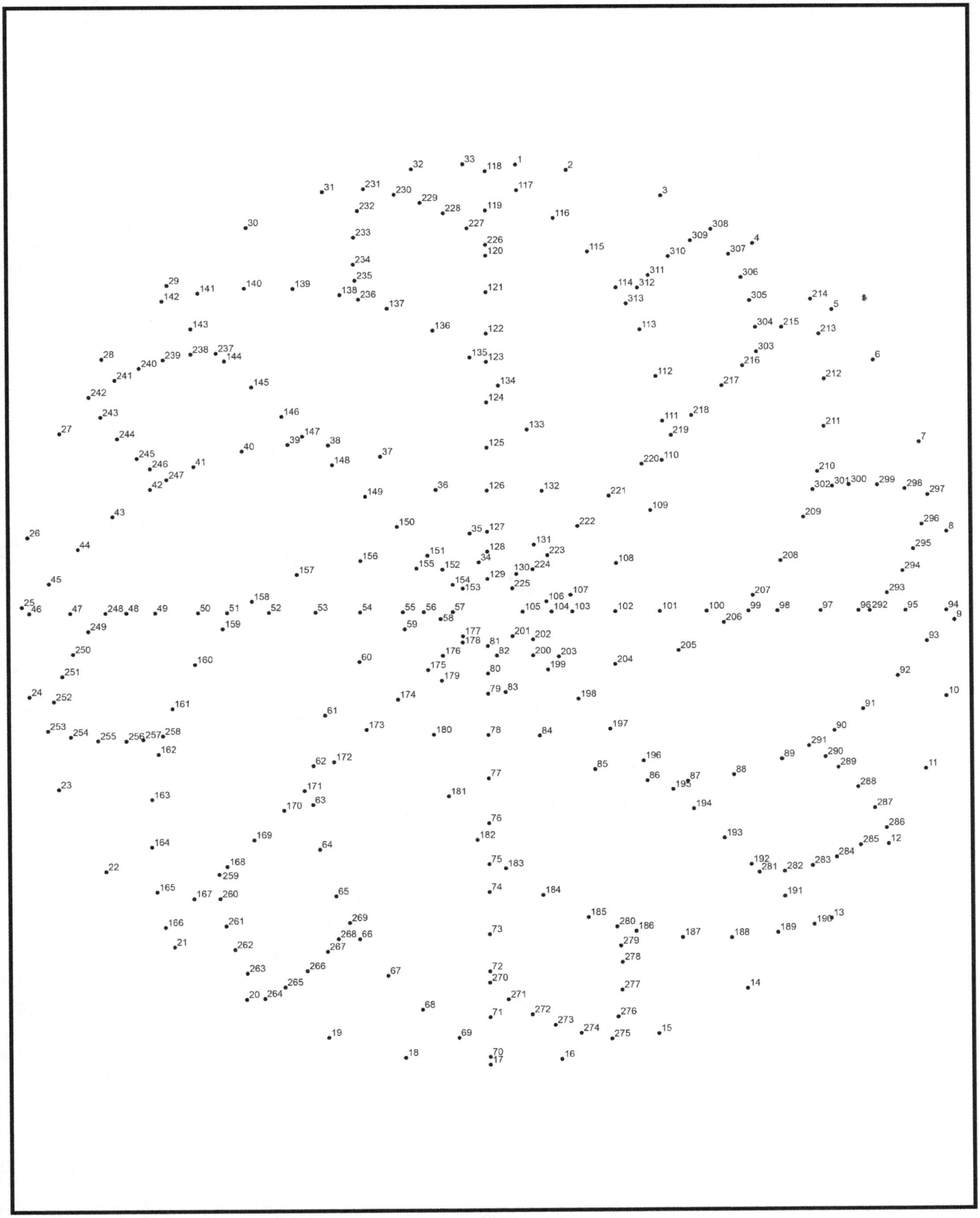

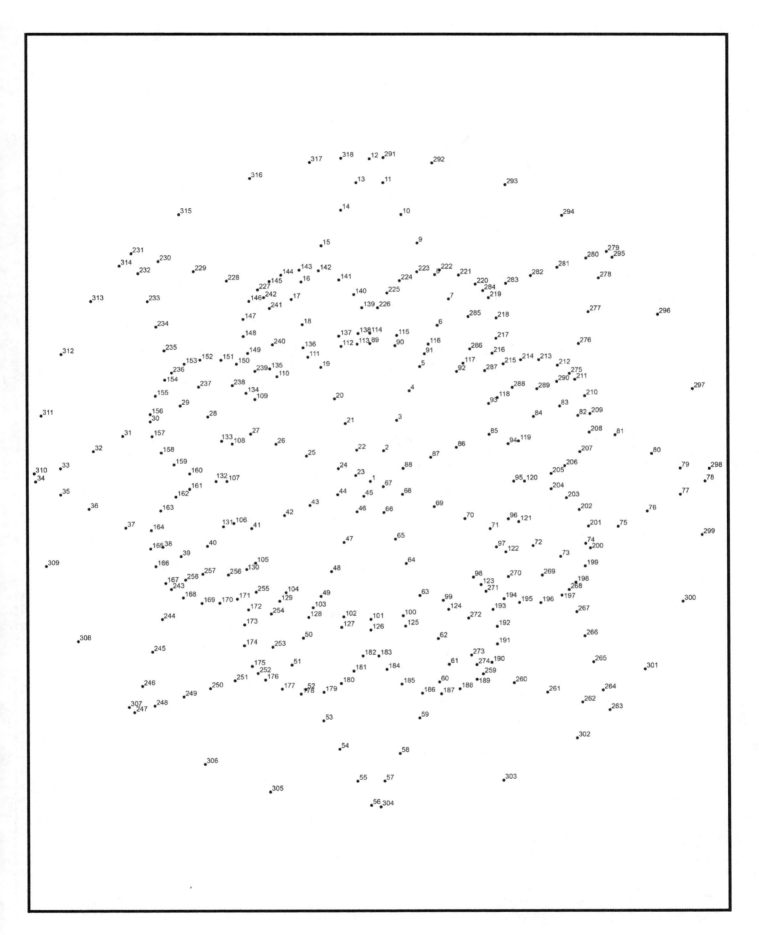

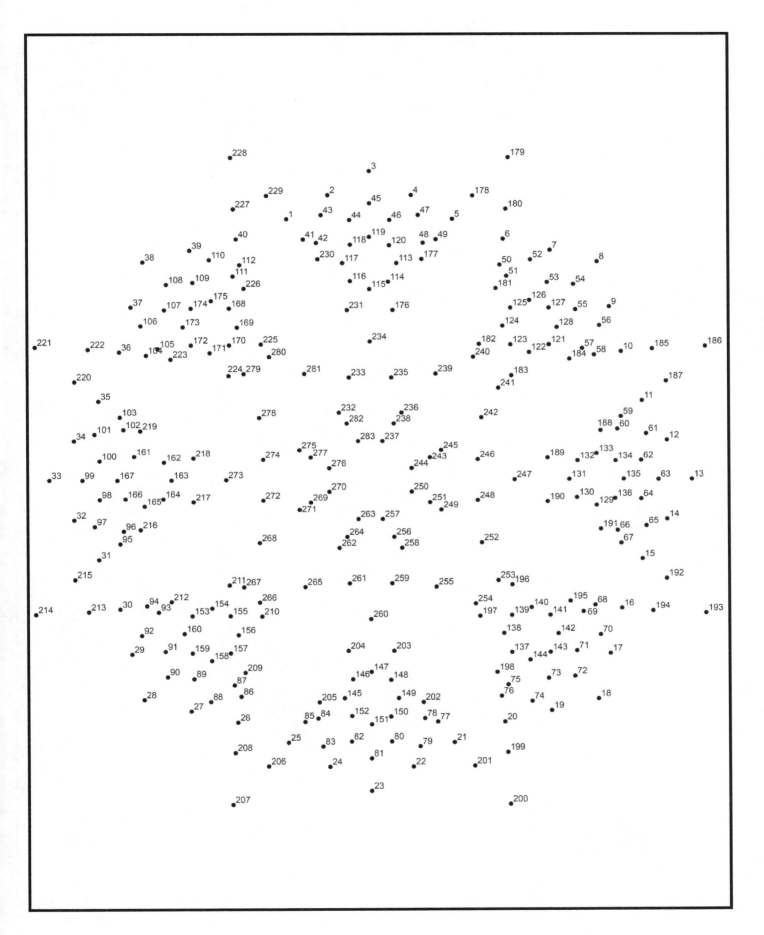

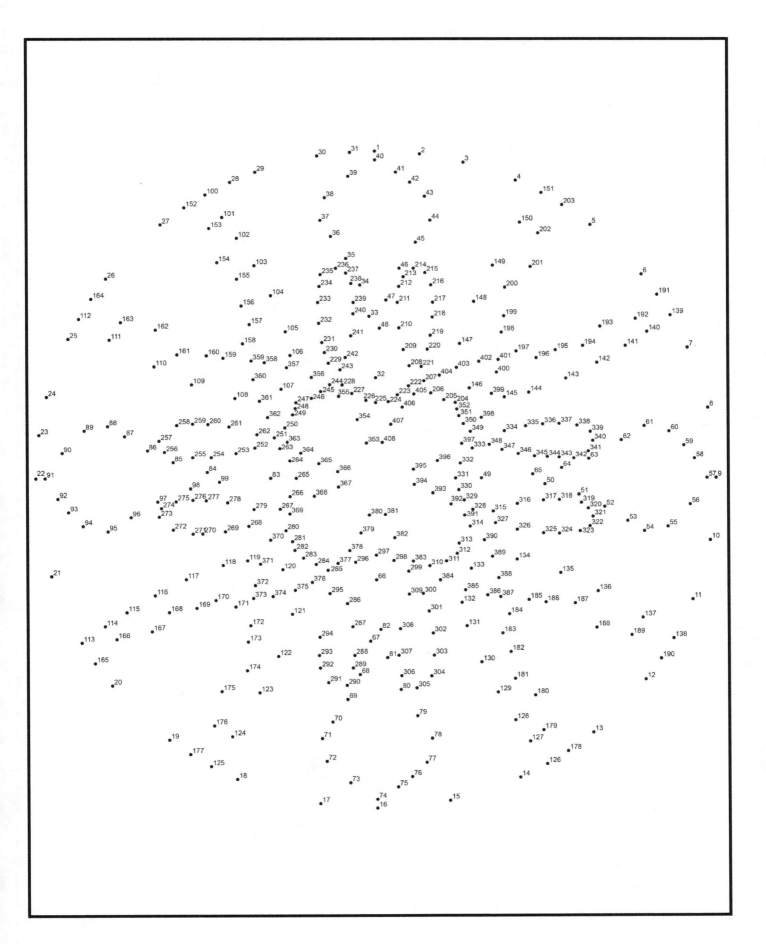

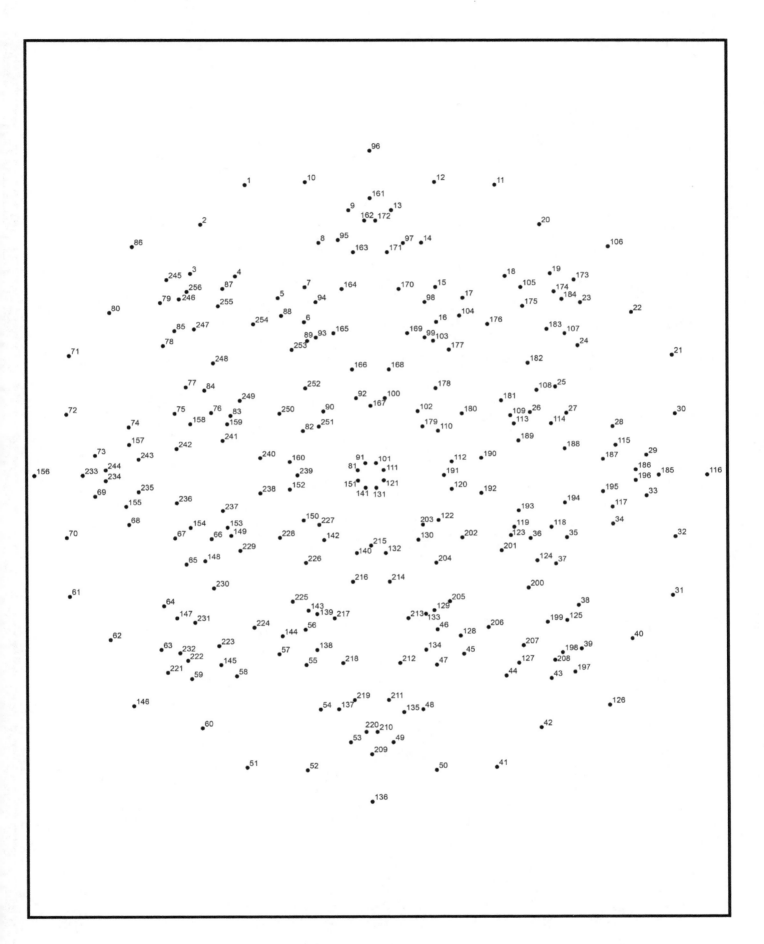

CPSIA information can be obtained
at www.ICGtesting.com
Printed in the USA
BVHW011230030121
596872BV00037B/1016